Twelve-year-old Jeff was delighted when he, and not his older brother Kurt, discovered the cave. All the Haley children immediately adopted it as a favorite setting for their cops-and-robbers games. But then a real bad guy entered the picture and Jeff learned that life is a lot more complicated than games.

JEFF and the
BAD GUY

JEFF and the BAD GUY

Written by Aleda Renkin
Art by Michael Norman

A Haley Adventure Book

Publishing House
St. Louis

Concordia Publishing House, St. Louis, Missouri
Copyright © 1973 Concordia Publishing House
Library of Congress Catalog Card No. 73-75863
ISBN 0-570-03602-X

CHAPTER 1

Kurt Haley was strong, handsome and smart, and no one knew it better than his younger brother Jeff. In fact, when Jeff was very small, he thought that was the way it was supposed to be in families. The younger brother was a sort of leftover deal. He still believed it when he started school and saw so many older brothers who were bigger, handsomer, and smarter than the younger ones. But he finally outgrew that idea, in fairness to his own younger brother who was only six. Donnie was a nice kid for being so young, and Jeff certainly was never going to be as bossy over Donnie as Kurt was over him.

There was also Pat, who was eleven, just thirteen months younger than Jeff, and was really surprisingly smart. Of course most girls do appear smarter at this age, Jeff told himself. He'd read that somewhere.

But Jeff wished more and more that he could do something to show Kurt that Jefferson Haley was brave and smart too, even if he wasn't handsome. He was getting a little tired of always being a sort of background to the smart brave things Kurt did. It wasn't that he didn't admire Kurt—he did very much. But he wanted to be admired too.

Then the big day came!

Ever since the Haley family moved to the country the children had been hiking over the bluffs and along the river. By now they thought they knew everything there was to know about the land their father had inherited. They loved the great feeling of space and room, especially since the place they had been living in the city had a yard only big enough for two sickly geraniums and one garbage can.

One summer afternoon they all sat on the edge of one of the highest bluffs and watched the river winding slowly through the valley below them. Donnie rolled over onto his stomach to peer over the edge of the rock cliff.

"Looky, there's another ledge right below this one," he informed them, wiggling further out on the edge of the bluff.

"That's far enough." Kurt grabbed Donnie's feet and jerked him back. "Do you want to fall down on those rocks below and break your neck?"

Donnie turned around, squinting pitifully. "Now look what you did, Kurt. You jerked me, and my glasses fell off."

"Oh, no, not again," Kurt groaned.

"We spend half our time looking for your specs," Pat scolded. "I hope you get your eyes corrected soon so you won't have to wear them any more."

"How can his eyes be corrected when half the time the glasses aren't where Donnie is?" asked Kurt.

Jeff looked at Kurt. "You *did* jerk him, so it's not his fault." He leaned over the bluff's edge. "I see them. Look, on that bush just below the second ledge. I don't even think they're broken."

"I guess I'll have to climb down to get them." Kurt rose slowly, taking time to give Donnie a hard stare.

But before he got to the ledge, Jeff had dug his fingers behind a deeply embedded rock and crawled over. He swung free for a moment, then dropped easily to the ledge below, grinning to himself because for once he had been quicker than Kurt. He studied the steep rocky hill below him to figure out how he could get the rest of the way to pick up the glasses before Kurt came down. Damp cool air from behind him made him turn curiously. Then he saw it.

A cave!

Jeff had read everything he could find about caves, but he had never been in one. And now before him was a big opening that surely must be a cave.

He ran to the wide hole in the rock and saw a large room. The ceiling was lost in dark-

ness and so was the back, but there was enough light to show him a good-sized room.

"Wheeeeeeeeee!" he yelled and then jumped as his voice echoed hollowly all around him. He ran back to the opening. "You won't believe this. You simply won't believe it!" he shouted.

"What?" Kurt's voice sounded bored.

"A cave! There's a real honest-to-goodness cave down here. It looks like a whopper." Jeff ran back inside, wishing he had a flashlight.

In a second Kurt had swung down to the rock shelf and was inside too. Jeff had disappeared in the blackness beyond the light from the opening.

"I'll bet this cave is under the whole bluff." Jeff's voice came back like he was talking through a big pipe.

"Jeff, you get back here," Kurt ordered, "It's dangerous to be exploring in the dark. You might walk into a deep hole."

Jeff emerged into the light. "I think I got to the back wall, but it's far back. Do you think Dad knew there was a cave on this property?"

"He'd have told us. After all, Dad didn't live here. He only visited his uncle once or twice. Gosh, I wish we had our flashlights. I'll bet there are stalactites on the roof of this cave."

"I want to come down!" Pat wailed from the top of the bluff. "Is it a walk-in cave?"

11

Kurt went outside. "It's a walk-in cave all right. Sit down and then push yourself, I'll catch you."

Pat sat down, closed her eyes because she hated heights, and slid. She knocked Kurt down when he caught her, but they were soon up and inside the cave.

"Hey, how about me—and Poochie?" Donnie called.

"I can catch him," Jeff said. "Donnie, jump and I'll catch you. Poochie has to wait for us up there."

As Jeff and his little brother entered the cave they heard Kurt say, "Here we can have our chance to play out those stories I write." His eyes were shining.

"We can whoop and holler all we want without making Mom mad." Donnie opened his mouth wide and gave a blood chilling yell that made them all jump—even Donnie himself.

"We can store some of our guns here so they won't be under Mom's feet all the time. We can bring flashlights and do some exploring—oh, gosh! It's too good to be true." Jeff ran his hands over some of the damp rocks. "Maybe there's even gold in here. Look how this glitters."

"You're getting carried away, Jeff," said Kurt. "If there had been gold here, someone would have discovered it years ago. But it's a great cave and I suppose it does belong to us and we can have some great times here."

They were so deep in plans for the games in the cave that they forgot about the time. When the cave grew darker, they looked outside and saw that the sun was just tipping the trees in the woods near the river.

"We've got to go," Pat said, "Mom will be worried."

But getting up to the next rock shelf stumped them for a while. Finally they found two big rocks that they rolled together. With Kurt on his tiptoes on the rocks, he could reach up and pull himself to the top.

"We'll bring a rope next time, and then it will be easy to slide up and down here," he said. "Now, Jeff, give Pat a boost and I'll lie down flat and grab her hands. Pat, you hold on to my wrists for dear life, hear?"

Pat had a bad moment when she felt her feet swing free, but Kurt got her wrists and she scrambled to the top. "Let's build an escalator!" she cried breathlessly, still a little pale.

Jeff turned to Donnie, who was sitting sadly on a big rock. "Now you."

"No use. I might as well stay and live here, and you can bring me a crust of bread once in a while," Donnie said sadly.

"What's wrong with you? We're late now. Stop acting so silly," Kurt called angrily.

"I can't go home without my glasses," Donnie said.

Jeff groaned but sat down and began to slide to the bush where the glasses hung. It was very steep and he had to grab at roots and rocks to keep from sliding down the rest of the bluff. He finally got to the bush, put the glasses safely in his pocket, and started the steep climb back. It was slow going because loose rocks slid out from under his feet, and sometimes he lost as much progress as he made.

When Jeff finally reached Donnie and they all got to the top of the bluff, the sun had gone down and there were already dark shadows in the woods below the bluffs. The fun of the discovery of the cave was a little dimmed when the children thought of Dad's being home before they got there. Dad had no patience with them when they worried their mother.

But Mr. Haley was late and Granny and Mrs. Haley were laughing over something funny that had happened while they were cooking dinner.

"We're sorry, Mom," Kurt said, as always the speaker of the house, "but Jeff discovered a cave, and we were so excited about it we forgot the time."

How nice that sounded to Jeff. *Jeff* had discovered a cave—not Kurt, no siree, not this time. *Jeff* had discovered it.

14

Mrs. Haley was spooning caramel sauce over brown crisp apple-dumplings. "Well, I should think a cave is enough to make you a little late. Tell me all about this wonderful cave."

"It's big and cool. It's on our property, so if a bomb falls we'll have a place to go . . ."

"Oh, Pat!" Kurt groaned.

"Anyway," continued Pat, "we couldn't see all of it because we had no flashlights and when Donnie hollered it *sounded* big."

"I'm sure it must be big if it *sounded* that way," sneered Kurt.

"I've heard churches that *sounded* big," Granny said quickly. Granny always tried to help Pat when the boys teased her. "Funny, I haven't thought about that cave for years, and so now you finally found it." Granny tasted the green beans and added some salt.

"You know about the cave?" Jeff asked in surprise.

"I saw it a few times — when I was young enough to swing over the ledge." Granny's eyes twinkled as if she loved remembering.

"You? You swung over that ledge?" Pat cried.

"You have to if you want to go into the cave, don't you?" Granny measured coffee into the percolator.

"Swing over a ledge? But that sounds

dangerous." Mrs. Haley's smile faded. "Did all of you get into the cave?"

"Kurt helped us. He. . . ." Pat stopped when Kurt frowned and shook his head at her.

Their father came in then, and all four children began talking at once about Jeff's exciting discovery.

During dinner Kurt explained how they had discovered it. Because he was excited, his voice sometimes was high and at other times an uncertain growl. Jeff wondered why Kurt always did the talking, even though he was so unsure of what kind of voice was coming out of his mouth. He made up his mind that when his own voice began to change, he would shut up and let someone else talk once in a while. Give Pat a chance. That was one nice thing about girls growing up. Their voices didn't do those crazy gymnastics. Of course, Pat was still far away from growing up.

"I don't like the idea of you children having to swing out on a bluff to get inside a cave. I'm not at all sure I want you to go there by yourselves." Mrs. Haley was slicing some bread that Granny had just taken from the oven.

There was a groan from all the children.

To Jeff that cave was one of the most important things that had happened to him for a long time.

"We'll take a rope and tie it to a tree and

slide down," he said. "There's nothing dangerous about that, is there? Oh, Dad, we've *got* to go
to that cave! I've always wanted to explore a
cave, and here we have one practically in our
back yard."

Mr. Haley smiled. "Not quite, son. If
it's in the highest bluff, it's pretty far away.
Ruth, if they slide down a rope, you won't have
to worry. I think they will be very careful and
it will be quite an adventure."

Donnie's eyes got big with wonder.
"Maybe some real live Indians live way down in
the insides of the cave."

Granny smiled. "About twenty years ago
some convicts escaped from the prison and holed
up in that cave for a week. They had food and
water that someone had stored there for them.
The police sure had a hard time getting them
out."

"Did the cops have to shoot them out?"
Kurt asked.

"No, they stunk them out with some sort
of chemical that made their eyes water. No one
got hurt because the convicts had no guns."

"I guess that proves that there's no other
way out of the cave," said Kurt. "Otherwise the
convicts could have gotten out."

"I suppose it's just that one big room,"
added Pat.

"But while I was in the back of the cave

I felt all around the wall, and there was a hole big enough to crawl into — so I thought there might be — "

Mr. Haley broke in sternly, looking at Jeff. "One thing I want to make clear right now. There will be *no* exploring. You are all to stay in the first room. I promise that soon we'll take a hike over there and have lanterns and flashlights along and then maybe, if I think it's safe, we can do a little exploring."

They all agreed, but Jeff was disappointed. He'd wanted so much to go see what was beyond that opening.

"Jeff, did you hear me?" Mr. Haley asked.

Jeff jumped. Funny how sometimes his dad seemed to read him. "Yes, sir."

CHAPTER 2

The Haley children went to the cave as often as they could get permission to be gone for several hours. It took them forty minutes to hike to the bluff, and once they got to the cave they could hardly pull themselves away.

Kurt liked to write stories for them to act out, and since they had the cave his imagination was really fired up. Wild westerns were his favorites. Donnie never got a very important role, and sometimes they argued over who'd play the main character, but the children always looked forward to the cave games.

They dug out all the play guns from the old toy box in the attic and even bought a few new ones when they had the money to spare. Donnie saved enough from his ice-cream-cone fund to buy a dandy pair of toy handcuffs that really locked. He was very proud of them and decided that no one could use them except himself, when Kurt let him play the smart sheriff or a real bad guy that was smart too.

The children tried not to talk about these games in front of their mother, but once she saw them gathering up some guns.

"Don't you see enough violence on television without playing it all the time?"

"We don't really get to see much violence, Mom. You always turn off the set when it gets exciting," Jeff said softly.

"And in our games the good guys always get the bad guys," Donnie added happily.

"I still don't see why you can't play something else . . . like . . . well, like . . ."

"Like what?" Pat prompted.

"Like ping-pong, or baseball."

"But ping-pong is an inside game, and you want us to get fresh air," Jeff said.

"The closest place to play baseball is at Kimball's, and that's three miles toward town," Kurt put in.

Mrs. Haley looked out the kitchen window. "You know, there's enough ground beyond the fence to have a small baseball diamond if you would just clear out all that buckbrush."

The Haley children did not seem to think too much of that idea. First of all, buckbrush was a stubborn old weed to get out. Also they figured they had enough work keeping the vegetable garden weeded and the lawn cut to say nothing of trimming the front hedge. Besides, Kurt's work at the drug store had been increased to twice a week and Jeff had three more customers on his paper route.

But most of all they had found Kurt's story games at the cave very exciting. Sometimes they got so wild, chasing around for the bad guy, that Jeff could hardly go to sleep at night. He never told anyone that. Oh my, how Kurt would have laughed!

"I just wish Sam were here. Wouldn't he get a kick out of that cave?" Kurt said one day as they were getting ready to hike to the cave.

"I guess Sam is seeing a lot more exciting things than a cave," Pat said wistfully. "Imagine traveling all over the United States with your dad and plenty of money."

"Does plenty of money make up for having no mother?" Kurt asked sternly.

"No, of course I didn't mean that," Pat said hurriedly. "I know Sam would rather his mother be alive and . . . but Granny loves him very much, and soon he'll be back here living with her again."

"Sam likes going to school here and living with Granny. He's told me so lots of times." Jeff tested his flashlight before he put it in the sack with the guns and ropes.

Mrs. Haley came to the basement, carrying an armload of clothes. "Not more guns? I suppose you think you're going to play cops and robbers at the cave again?" Mrs. Haley began sorting out clothes.

"You said we could," Pat said meekly.

"When?"

"I asked this morning when you were talking on the phone to Granny about that

quilting thing. I asked you if we could go to the cave and you nodded."

Mrs. Haley looked cross. "You know very well how hard it is to concentrate when two people are talking to you. I don't remember your asking me at all, as you probably know."

"But we've got everything packed, and we've done all the things you told us to do around the house," Kurt said reproachfully.

"I don't like these gun games at all. You know that. I don't think your father realizes how much of your playtime is used up with that sort of thing since you discovered the cave. I think we will have to have a family court session soon."

Their faces fell. A court session would most certainly knock out the games at the cave.

"May we go just for a little while?" Donnie begged.

Mrs. Haley looked thoughtful. "For one hour."

"But Mom, we'll have to turn back as soon as we get there. One hour is nothing when you have to hike so far," Kurt protested.

"If you would sometime let us spend a whole day, maybe we could get the whole thing out of our systems." Jeff was proud of his speech. He had sounded so reasonable, so adult.

Mrs. Haley's face brightened.

"That might be a good idea. Maybe playing around in that damp cool cave for a whole day *would* cure you. I know a good day for you to do it, too — when the quilters are here."

"Quilters? What's that?" Donnie asked.

"Quilters. Don't act so stupid. Quilters are women who sew up things you use to cover with on beds when you don't have electric blankets," Pat explained.

"Remember when we mowed Granny's grass, we saw her cutting up little bits of material? Well, after they're all cut up you sew them together again and that's quilting." Jeff was trying to get his mother's mind off the guns.

"First you cut them up, then you sew them together again?" Donnie began to laugh.

"This is not a joke, Donald," Mrs. Haley said severely. "The Ladies Auxiliary gets together twice a year and makes a nice warm quilt to give to the old people's rest-home. I think it's a lovely thing to do."

"But why cut it up if you're going to sew it together again?" Donnie persisted.

Pat saw that her mother was getting angry, so she said quickly, "Did you tell Granny that you would ask the quilters to spend the day here?"

"Yes, the day after tomorrow. They come early in the morning and stay until the quilt is finished. They eat breakfast, lunch, and supper here."

"That would be a great day to be gone," Kurt said. "We could pack up our lunch, and you wouldn't have to worry about us all day long."

"Just one minute. I'll let you have the whole day then, but it means that you'll have to work hard tomorrow getting the place in order and helping me cook and bake for the next day. I do want everything to look spick and span, and I want my food to be good. Granny will be here to help me bake too."

The children were so excited about having an entire day at the cave that they recklessly promised to work hard all day tomorrow without grumbling.

CHAPTER 3

They soon found out what Mrs. Haley meant by "spick and span." She meant dusting and polishing every single inch of the house — even the darkest corners. She meant doing the lawn and the porches and even the basement.

"Who are these 'quilters' anyway? Are they some sort of inspectors that we have to be so clean?" Kurt was clipping grass around the big oaks on the lawn.

Jeff turned off the motor of the mower and rested his arms on the handle. "If they have to cut up all the little pieces so they can sew them together again, when will they have time to poke their noses in the back corners of the hall closet — or open all the doors in the kitchen cabinets?"

They both laughed and Pat came across the lawn, stopping to pick up a tiny bit of paper. "Boys, get it all nice and clean," she said grinning.

"And what have you been doing for the Great Cause?" Kurt asked.

"I dusted everything, and I mean *everything*. I scrubbed the bathrooms, and now I'm going in to devil some eggs."

"What's Donnie doing?"

"He's manicuring Poochie's toenails."

The boys roared so loud that Mrs. Haley looked out the window. "Boys, are you wasting time? We still have many things to do."

"What other things? What could be left to do?" Kurt muttered under his breath.

"I heard you, Kurt Haley. Stop grumbling. Remember you've got the entire day to play tomorrow." Her face disappeared from the window, then was back again. "The eggs are cool enough to devil now, Pat."

"I'm coming." Pat ran to the kitchen.

"Guess I'm ready for the next orders." Kurt wiped off the clipping shears with his shirttail. "I wouldn't be one bit surprised if we didn't have to scrub the road in front of the house."

Jeff grinned. "We're earning our tomorrow, remember. His eyes sparkled. "Say, I like that. 'We pay for our yesterdays and earn our tomorrows.' Who said that beside me?"

He turned on the lawn mower again so he didn't hear what Kurt said, but he knew it wasn't very flattering anyway.

That evening Granny came over, and they moved all the dusted furniture out of the dining room and erected a quilting frame so big that there was only enough room to put chairs around it. After that was done, Granny and Mrs.

Haley frosted some cakes and set dough for fresh sweet rolls for breakfast.

"Those quilters must really have appetites," Kurt commented to his father when Granny finally left.

Mrs. Haley came back in the kitchen. There were frown wrinkles in her forehead. "Please don't eat out of the company dishes. Eat leftovers. I don't want to run out of food."

"Now, honey, you've got enough food in this house to feed all of India," Mr. Haley said gently. "Why do you wear yourself out on a thing like a bunch of women coming to sew on a quilt?"

"But I've never had them before, Bill, and I do want things to be nice."

"How can they be otherwise? Now, you go upstairs and take a relaxing bath and I'll bring you a glass of hot milk. What time do they come in the morning?"

"Awfully early. Maybe seven," Mrs. Haley said apologetically.

Mr. Haley winked at Kurt. "I've got to get to work for an early appointment tomorrow. I'll just grab a cup of coffee and a roll at the joint across from the office."

Jeff awoke the next morning to the sound of women's chatter. He saw Kurt in the next bed, leaning on his elbow, his eyes heavy with sleep.

"Would you believe the 'quilters' are here

already?" he said drowsily.

"Guess we'd better get up. Remember the orders—all beds made nice and smooth. No clothes thrown around."

Jeff leaped out of bed and began dressing. "Come on, get up! The sooner we get up, the sooner we can get out of here. The house belongs to the 'quilters.' "

As the boys passed the dining room they saw several women already hunched around the quilt. Mrs. Haley was serving coffee and hot sweet rolls. Granny was in the kitchen scrambling eggs for Pat and Donnie.

"I was about to call you. Serve yourself orange juice, and I'll make more eggs and toast."

"How about some of those orange rolls Mom was passing around to the quilters?" Kurt asked.

"Your mother said to make you toast," Granny said firmly and popped some bread into the toaster. "Cheer up, maybe there'll be a lot of goodies left when you get home from the cave."

Jeff was wolfing down cereal. "Pat, wait until you hear the great story Kurt wrote last night. It's the best yet."

"I hope he gives me a part where I can say something. Mostly I just have to tag around behind the sheriff like a dummy." Donnie tried to wipe the egg yolk off his clean shirt.

"That's what deputies are supposed to do." Kurt laughed and reached for the plate of eggs. "When you get real smart and tough, you can be a sheriff. Thanks, Granny, you're a good kid."

Pat and Jeff were often shocked at the way Kurt talked to Granny, but she seemed to like it, and they knew that Kurt adored Granny.

The children cleaned up the kitchen, and Granny went in to quilt. All the chairs were taken, and there was a constant chatter of ladies' voices.

"They've already cut the things up and sewed them again," Donnie reported after a trip to the dining room. "Now, why are they all sitting around and sewing some more?"

"I guess you'll never know until you're old enough to be a quilter," answered Pat. "Now, all you guys make your own sandwiches. And I'm warning you, don't use anything that Mom has made for her luncheon. There's left-over stuff from supper and cheese and peanut butter, and that's it. We can have cookies and I'll make lemonade, but I've got to straighten up my room first. Then let's get out of here. Did you ever hear so much talking in your whole life?"

"Yes," Kurt said, "when you had a slumber party on your birthday."

Mrs. Haley came into the kitchen. She

already looked a little tired. "Be sure and be home by five," she cautioned and put on another pot of coffee. "I do hope I don't run out of coffee." She didn't seem to be talking to anyone special, so the children began packing up their gear. It amounted to quite a bit, and they looked like an African safari when they finally started down the path through the woods.

Soon they came to the creek. There was only a trickle of water in it, but it was enough to make the rocks slippery, and with all the things they had to carry, it took them quite a while to cross. They had just reached the thick woods on the other side when they heard a loud humming noise above them. They were sur-prised to see a helicopter flying low over the woods and hills ahead.

"Say, this isn't in my story," said Kurt, "but wouldn't it be fun to pretend there are cops in that copter that are looking for us? Let's keep out of their sight." He ran for the cover of the trees.

It was an exciting game. When there was an open space they had to cross, they waited until the copter was over another part of the woods. They couldn't take the usual route over the fields but stayed in the woods and climbed the bluffs. This was a much harder route and took them twice the time.

At the top of the first hill they had to stop

and rest. The helicopter was still circling, but the children were under a thick cluster of cedars.

"Wonder why they keep staying around here," said Pat.

"Maybe they really are looking for someone who got lost," Jeff suggested.

"Who would they be looking for?" asked Kurt. "There are no little kids around here to get lost. I'll bet it's just one of the state patrolmen giving a new cop some driving lessons."

"It's been fun hiding from them. You think we can get in the cave without them seeing us?" Pat asked.

"Oh, they'll be gone by that time," said Kurt. "Let's get going."

Kurt was right. By the time they got to the big bluff, the copter was nowhere in sight. He tied a strong rope to a nearby tree, and it was no time at all before they and all their equipment were inside the cave. By now Pat was so good at rope-sliding that she took Poochie down in her arms.

"I wish we'd left that dumb dog at home," Kurt muttered. "He always manages to give away our hiding places."

"We can pretend he's one of those killer dogs the police use sometimes," suggested Pat.

"I haven't got that in the story," Kurt said firmly, and took out some sheets of paper covered with writing.

32

"I'm hungry. Let's eat first," said Donnie.

"It's too early," Kurt told him. "Sit down and I'll read the story to you."

They sat in a circle on the damp rocks just inside the cave, and Kurt began to read. Above the bluff they could hear the hum of the helicopter again.

"I still think it's awfully funny, that helicopter passing over these woods all the time," Pat said.

"Do you want to hear the rest of the story, or do you want to talk about the helicopter?" Kurt glared at her and she shrugged and said nothing.

Kurt turned another page. "Now, get this! The crook in this story is really bad business. He's hidden the stolen money in a cave, but he's too smart to let them find it. He's so smart he can just about get away from anyone. He . . ."

"That's for me!" Donnie shrilled. "I can play that part real good."

"No you can't," Kurt snapped.

"I can too. Besides I'm sick of being the dumb deputy. The sheriff always gets the bad guy and the deputy watches and does nothing. I'm tired of just watching! I'm sick of being good! I want to be the bad, *bad* guy."

"Oh, let him be the bad guy once. I'll be the watching deputy," Jeff said impatiently.

"We don't have a deputy this time. In

my story he broke his leg the day before yesterday."

"Oh, but that's 'violence,' isn't it?" asked Donnie.

Kurt groaned. "Donnie, I'm just kidding. Now, will you please just listen? In this story there are *two* bad guys. That will be you and me, and you've got to be *tough*. You can't be whining about a scratched knee or being tired when we're running to hide in the woods. Is that clear?"

"Don't worry about me being tough." Donnie made such a ferocious face, that Pat had to turn her head to hide a smile.

"Jeff and Pat can be the two cops who are after us, and we'll try not to give them but one clue as to which direction we went."

Kurt went on with the story, and since Jeff had heard it twice before, he got up and wandered to the back of the cave. He wanted to flash his light down that low doorway at the back of the cave. He had done that before on their other trips to the cave, but there was something about the steep rough drop into the blackness below that always gave him a fearful sort of thrill.

Where did it go? Did it end in a deep hole, or did it go on and on? Did it come out on the other side of the bluff, or did it end up by the river? How Jeff wished he could explore it! That

would be a lot more fun than playing cops and robbers.

He backed away from the hole and turned off his flashlight. It struck him suddenly that there was a dead silence at the front of the cave where his brothers and sister were. He turned and saw them still sitting there. But they were frozen into statues, facing the opening of the cave. The rope still hung there, but it was beginning to move, as if someone on top of the bluff was handling it! Then it began to jiggle and shake and a pair of feet slid down, followed by long khaki-covered legs. In a second a figure stood outlined against the light.

CHAPTER 4

Jeff didn't move one muscle. There was something frightening in the way that tall figure blocked the cave. This was no game. Poochie started toward the figure, barking wildly.

"Shut him up." The stranger spoke softly, but Jeff heard every word.

Donnie seemed frozen with fear, so Pat made a grab for the pup and petted it to silence. Because the man's back was to the light, they couldn't see his face, but he seemed young. He stepped further into the cave and pulled something from his pocket. It gleamed briefly in the light. It was a knife, an odd thing that could have been made out of almost any kind of metal.

Jeff pressed against the back wall, trying to think, wishing he knew what to do.

"Now, you kids keep quiet." For all their softness, the words sounded threatening.

None of the three had made a sound; they seemed hardly to be breathing.

Suddenly there was the hum of the helicopter again, and the man's hand holding the knife motioned toward the sky. "They know you're here?"

"Who?" Kurt asked.

"The cops." The strange voice sounded tense.

"How do you know they're cops?" Jeff was proud of the cool calm way Kurt talked.

"Don't act dumb! You know they're cops. I want to know if they saw you come in here." He came nearer to Kurt, but Kurt did not shrink back.

Then Jeff remembered with a sinking heart how they had played the game of hiding from the men in the helicopter. What a stupid game it had been! If they had not played it, the police would soon be in the cave and whoever the stranger . . .

Pat was talking, ". . . and who are you and what right have you to talk to us like that? This is our cave!"

"Shut up!" the man said fiercely. "I don't think the cops saw you, or they'd have landed on that cleared space above here. I know they couldn't see your rope, because I almost missed it myself." He stood silent for a while, then he spoke in an oily smooth voice. "I think the best thing I can do for a while is just visit with you till the cops start looking some other place."

The helicopter sounded far in the distance, and the man stepped further into the cave and surveyed the three. "So you're the tough guy of the bunch," he said to Donnie. "I'm tough too, kid."

Donnie didn't look very tough. He looked like he was about to cry.

The man peered into the darkness beyond the light thrown from the front of the cave. "Where's the other one?"

Jeff's heart skipped a beat, and for a second he had the wild idea of crawling back into the dark opening behind him.

The man nudged Kurt with his foot. "Where's the other guy? I know he's here somewhere. I heard him talk while you were reading your stinking baby story. A big hunk like you writing and playing cops and robbers!" He laughed hard with a sting that made Kurt flinch.

"Hey, you, come out! I know you're back there somewhere," the stranger called softly.

Jeff didn't move. If the man came looking for him, it would give Kurt a chance to shinny up the rope and run for help or flag down the helicopter. Then the stranger spotted Kurt's flashlight.

"Kick that over to me," he ordered.

Never taking his eyes from the three, he picked it up and turned it on. In a second Jeff was blinded by the light.

"Playing hide-and-go-seek, wise guy? Now come out and sit down with the rest of the kids."

Jeff moved slowly forward and sat down by Donnie.

"Now, we'll just stay here nice and cozy until it's almost dark. No one can find anyone in these woods at night."

"How do you know so much about these woods? You've been . . ." Pat stopped at the sudden flash of anger in the man's eyes.

"Let's just be polite and say it's none of your business. Now suppose you just sit here nice and quiet, and that way you'll stay out of trouble. You can all be the 'good guys' and," he nodded to Donnie, "the 'big shot' and I will be the bad guy." That seemed funny to him and he gave a hard laugh. Then he sat down just inside the cave, half facing them.

For the first time they could see his face and were surprised at how young he looked— almost a boy. He kept sharp eyes on all of them, but when he looked at Donnie his eyes softened.

"Hey, you!" He said it so suddenly that they all jumped. He pointed to Donnie. "You stand up, crook, and drop your gun. I know it's loaded."

Donnie stood up, pale as ashes, unbuckled his gun belt, and let it drop in the best western-movie style. The stranger chuckled.

"So now that the toughest crook is un-armed, we can have a party. Anyone for pinning the tail on the donkey?" He looked at Kurt with a sneer. "That sounds about your style."

The muscles in Kurt's jaws worked furiously, and Jeff hoped he wouldn't fly into one of his rages and try to rush the stranger. Kurt was big and strong for his age, but no match for this guy. But Kurt didn't move.

Time dragged on endlessly, and the four Haleys sat stiff and damp on the cave floor. After a while the stranger got up and paced back and forth in front of the cave door. "What gets me is why you dumb kids came out in these hills at all today. The radio station has been broadcasting about me all morning." He pulled back his shoulders proudly. "Yes, sir, they gave me prime time."

No one said a word, and that angered him.

"Answer me! Don't you have a radio at your home?"

Pat finally answered. "Of course we have a radio."

"Then why didn't you turn it on? I'm an escaped. convict, see—I could be dangerous." He looked at each face in turn, watching for fear or horror.

"I don't believe you," Pat said firmly, trying to hide the way-down-deep trembling inside. "How could you hear about yourself on the radio if you were hiding in the woods?"

"You're a smart-aleck, kid. I had a transistor, and I listened to the whole thing. The cops were always looking in the wrong places." He gave that hard laugh that had no fun in it at all. "Gosh, those cops are stupid!"

"Where's the transistor now?" Jeff asked.

"Fell out of my pocket when I slid down the rope. It's somewhere down on those rocks, but I don't dare go out to get it. It busted anyways, I guess."

"They'll find you, you know. The helicopter's been out over the woods all morning," Jeff said, surprised at himself.

The convict studied him. "I don't think so, buddy. If they'd seen you, they'd be down here questioning you, and if they didn't see *four,* how could they see one?"

"Because . . ." Donnie began, but Pat gave him such a hard pinch that he jumped and screamed.

"Never mind him," Pat said quickly. "He gets funny fits when he has to sit quiet for too long. You'd better let him walk around a little."

"Walk around then, but don't ever yell like that again." The convict was still startled.

"Don't you dare tell him anything," Pat whispered as she pulled Donnie to his feet. "Just don't talk at all. Act dumb."

"Just walk one at a time," the convict ordered, and Pat sat down again.

So they took turns, trying to get the cold

stiffness from their joints. The convict never took his eyes off them, and he still held the homemade-looking knife in his hand.

Donnie sat down near his lunch sack and tried to wiggle his hand closer to the bag.

"What's with you, kid? You going to have another fit?" the stranger asked.

"I want my lunch. I'm hungry," Donnie said pitifully.

"Lunch?" The convict's eyes traveled around the circle and saw that they each had a brown paper sack. "All of you just toss those nice little brown bags over to me," he ordered.

Donnie threw his sack last, his eyes looking longingly at it. The children watched the convict eat Pat's cheese sandwich, then Kurt's cold hamburgers. Next he picked up Jeff's fat meatloaf sandwich.

"Not bad," he said, wiping his lips with the back of his hand. "You kids hungry?"

"Oh, yes, sir," Donnie said politely, looking at his own paper bag. He thought that surely by now the convict would no longer be hungry.

The convict watched Donnie and then very slowly picked up the last bag and looked inside.

"Too bad, tough guy, but you see I figure you had a breakfast this morning. You had egg. I see it on your shirt."

"But that was so long . . ."

"Well, I didn't have *anything*. I didn't have a supper last night either, because I was hiding in a smelly sewer. Right about that time you were all sitting at a table with a lace cloth and napkins. Eating roast beef and gravy, right?"

"No lace and we had meat loaf," replied Donnie. "Listen, you won't like my sandwich because no one ever does. I made it myself." Donnie's voice was hopeful.

The stranger took the sandwich out of the bag. He watched Donnie. "I've got to eat it because I've got to know what toughies eat." A big glob of jelly oozed out of the sandwich and slid down his chin to his shirt. "Ooooophs! This *is* a lousy mess! Meat loaf and jelly!" But he finished the sandwich anyway.

"Now, hand over the jug," he ordered, and Jeff pushed the thermos nearer. The convict drank in big loud thirsty gulps.

After that he didn't talk for a while and the children occupied themselves with their own gloomy thoughts. Now was the time to pray, Jeff thought. He looked at Pat and somehow knew that she was having a very satisfying talk with God. Kurt looked like he was hatching up a great scheme to rescue them without praying. Donnie looked tired and hungry and very sorry for himself.

But it didn't really seem right for Jeff to pray. He remembered how many times he had prayed at the table, at night, or in church and hadn't paid attention to one word he'd said or thought. It seemed awfully cheap to rattle off a lot of words most of the time and only mean his prayers when he was really in trouble. No, he couldn't make himself believe God would pay too much attention to a part-time believer like him. He'd let Pat do the praying. There was no doubt about it, Pat stood in a lot better with God than he did.

The helicopter was hovering right above the bluff again. The convict got up, and his head jerked nervously while he listened. Finally the noise faded.

"I don't know how you found out about this cave," Kurt said. "But it's really no secret at all. There are people in town who know about it. They're sure to tell the cops and they'll find it."

"They won't find me here. What time is it?"

"Four-thirty."

"We're supposed to be home at five. Our mother will be expecting us," Pat put in.

The convict was eyeing the rope, and he said as if to himself, "I have to keep you kids from climbing up and waving down that heli-

copter." He turned to Kurt. "Cut down the rope, big mouth."

"I'll have to use your knife," Kurt said, white with fury.

"Oh, no, you don't. Skip it. I have no time to fool." With quick smooth movements the convict snatched a length of rope from where the guns were piled. Before Kurt knew what was happening, he was lying on the cave floor, his hands and feet tied together. Also, without Jeff's actually seeing how it happened, the convict had on Kurt's wristwatch. Then he glanced at Pat. "I don't think you could get up that rope with your hands tied," he said, and in a second had them fastened behind her.

Next he saw Donnie's handcuffs. "Here, kid, this ought to hold you for a while," he said, snapping them on. It was then that Donnie saw Kurt's wristwatch.

"You can't take that watch! That's stealing!" Donnie cried in horror.

"No, I'm just going to borrow it for a while. Now, you keep that dog quiet or I'll come back and he'll never bark again." He stopped to listen. Far off they could hear the barking of dogs. The convict threw Jeff a flashlight.

"Come on, let's head out!"

"Head out?" Jeff's heart skipped several beats. He knew what the convict meant.

"Out the back way, that hole you came out of when I first got here."

"I never came out that hole. I was just looking down in it. I don't know where it goes. My dad says it's dangerous to explore."

"You're lying. If this is your property like the kid said, you *must* have explored. Come on, I've no time to waste."

"He's *not* lying! He's never been in that hole at all!" Kurt shouted.

"Shut up, big mouth. Write us a nice little ending to this story and . . ." He stopped to listen. There was no doubt about it. There were dogs near. Poochie was shivering with fear. The boy swung around and ran to the back of the cave. The helicopter was right above them, its motor so loud that no one could have heard Kurt's yells or the dog's barking.

Jeff stayed right behind the convict, who turned and gave one last piercing look at him. "You never have been down there?" There was pleading and desperation in his voice.

"I never have."

Pat was behind Jeff. "Please don't go down. You might fall and be terribly hurt. The police will catch you anyway. We'll talk to the police. We'll tell them you didn't hurt us one bit. . . ."

But the convict wasn't listening. He was already in the hole. He sat down, holding the light before him, and began to slide down the slippery steep rocks. The steady rattle of pebbles followed his passage. He wasted no time, allowing himself to slide swiftly, only now and then trying to slow his speed by digging his heels in some rock holes or grabbing at jutting ledges on the dripping rock walls beside him. Soon he was just a dim light far below.

"I should have gone with him," Jeff worried.

"I don't see what you could have done," said Pat.

There was a sudden faint yell from far below, then a crashing of rocks that echoed and echoed. Jeff leaned as far forward as he dared.

"Are you all right? Hey! Please! Are you hurt?"

But only a few rolling rocks broke the quiet of the blackness below.

CHAPTER 5

Jeff stood horrified and stared down into the slice of light his small flashlight made in the plunging passageway. There was no sign of the convict.

"I'll run back and untie Kurt so he can get on top of the bluff and flag down the helicopter. They're staying close by," Pat said. Her hands were free, the rope lying at her feet.

"Who . . . who untied you?" Jeff asked in a daze.

"The rope came untied without my half trying. I don't think he really meant to tie me up at all. Gosh, I hope he isn't hurt badly."

"Where is he?" Donnie came running up. "Did he get down?"

"We think he fell," Pat said, as Jeff stood there looking into the hole. "Come on, let's untie Kurt so he can get the cops. They'll find a doctor, Jeff."

"I can't help untie Kurt. I don't know what happened to the key to my handcuffs," Donnie complained.

"Jeff, do you know where the key could be? Jeff, what are you going to do?" Pat's voice became shrill with fear.

"I've got to go down there," Jeff said, crawling in the opening.

"You can't help him anyway. You're no doctor. Jeff, someone will go down there soon. Please, you know it's dangerous!" Pat pulled at his arm.

Jeff jerked free. "I've *got* to go to him. I know he must be hurt."

"But you can't help him. Jeff, wait until we get help."

"I'm going. I wouldn't let a hurt dog down there in that blackness. How could I leave a human being, a boy? Get back to Kurt. Tell someone to bring a doctor and some kind of stretcher."

Slowly Jeff started to slide down the slippery rocks, holding the flashlight in one hand and trying to slow down his progress with the other. Whenever he found a ledge that seemed safe, he stopped and called but received no answer. He didn't look back but kept sliding downward into the blackness. His flashlight made a small pool of light right ahead of him, but otherwise the darkness seemed almost to smother him. He didn't realize that he was praying with all his heart.

Then suddenly he saw a sprawled figure in the pool of light below him. One leg was twisted back at such an angle that Jeff knew it was broken. The convict's face was covered with yellow clay and his eyes were closed. He lay

close to the edge of a wide chasm that Jeff's flashlight showed only the top of. It could have been bottomless.

The convict looked dead! Jeff almost panicked, but he knew he had to go the rest of the way. When he reached the convict he saw his eyes flutter. Then they opened, dull with shock and pain, and looked at Jeff.

"I'm going to have to try to move you closer to the wall," Jeff said softly.

"Just let me alone," the boy said through stiff lips.

"I'll have to move you. You're just inches away from a hole that looks like it has no bottom. I'll be very careful."

Slowly Jeff moved the boy's shoulders and the upper part of his body. Then he lifted the legs. The broken one almost made him sick. The convict moaned softly.

"I wish I had something to give you for the pain, but someone will be here soon."

The boy didn't answer and Jeff pulled off his shirt and held it under a dripping trickle of water. Gently he washed most of the yellow clay from the boy's drawn face. "You slipped and fell?"

The boy nodded and opened his eyes again. "Why did you come down?"

"Because you were alone. Because I knew you were hurt."

"Crazy!" The boy just barely whispered it, then closed his eyes again. Jeff sat silently, watching the drawn face.

He lost all sense of time until a brilliant light suddenly pierced the blackness. "Jeff, are you all right?"

It was his father's voice. Jeff felt like he could slide right up that golden beam.

"I'm fine, Dad, but the boy's hurt bad. He's got a broken leg and I don't know what else is wrong."

"A doctor is coming down now on a rope ladder. As soon as he gets there, you climb up. We'll have plenty of help down there soon."

Jeff came out of the hole, covered with sticky yellow clay, his eyes blinking from all the blazing lights in the cave.

"I hope he just fainted. He wouldn't answer me any more."

"They'll fix him up, put him under, then take him to a hospital," said Mr. Haley gently.

A man in a uniform came up with pad and pencil. "I'd like to have a full report."

They all looked at Jeff, and he was glad the mud hid some of the redness he could feel on his face. He told the story quickly, anxious to get it over.

"Can't he fill in the details later?" Mr. Haley asked. "These kids' mother is at home sick with worry, and I'd like to get them home as soon as possible.

The officer nodded. "I'll come out later."

Jeff nudged his father. "I'd like to stay to see how he is, Dad, please."

"I'll stay here and find out, then tell you about him when I get home. Now a trooper will take you kids right home.

The ride home in the jeep was thrilling but a little frightening, especially since it was completely dark by now. The sight of their house with every window a blaze of light and their mother running out to meet them was joy complete.

Mrs. Haley listened to the story of the convict, her eyes wide with horror, she didn't seem quite convinced that none of her children had been hurt. She said none of the ladies had paid much attention to the helicopter that afternoon and hadn't even thought of turning on the radio until Mr. Head, the rural mail carrier, came by and told them they'd better be sure to have their car keys out of the ignition because a convict was supposed to be hiding somewhere near the neighborhood.

No sooner had the women all gone when Mr. Haley came home, followed by a jeep with four officers. Since only Granny knew for sure how to get to the cave, she rode in the jeep with the police. She said afterward it was like riding a billy goat barebacked down the Grand Canyon.

Jeff could hardly wait for his father to get home again. He chilled with fear whenever he thought of the boy's face, dead white under the clay.

"How is he?" Jeff asked anxiously as soon as Mr. Haley walked in.

"He had a bad fracture, maybe some broken ribs. They can't be sure until they make some tests. By now he's in the hospital and well taken care of."

"And we're starving. Oh, my goodness, Donnie, haven't you found those handcuff keys yet?" Pat exclaimed. I'll bet they're upstairs under your bed. That's where all your stuff ends up."

"Sure!" said Donnie. "Now I remember." He disappeared up the stairs and reappeared almost immediately with a triumphant smile and the keys.

Pat unlocked the handcuffs and tossed them in the garbage can. "That's that!" she said firmly.

"And that goes for the guns too," said Kurt. "I've had enough cops and robbers for the rest of my life. Say, Dad, how did that kid get in prison anyway?"

"He stole a car. It's really sad because he was eligible for a parole in five months."

"I guess five months just seemed endless to him," Jeff said, seeing again the boy's desperate eyes as he crawled in the hole.

"Still you just can't go around stealing cars and not be punished," Pat said.

"Well, I'm proud of my son. That was a fine thing to do, Jeff, to go down into that hole. It took a lot of courage," Mr. Haley said.

"I didn't do any good, Dad. He fainted soon after I got to him, and I don't think it meant a thing to him to have me there."

"I wouldn't be too sure," Pat said. "Anyway, you didn't know for sure that he was hurt before you went down. He might have been down there waiting to clobber you, but you went anyway."

"If he wanted to hurt us, he had all day to do it. Besides, you said yourself he really didn't tie you up at all—the rope just fell off your wrists. What he wanted was to get away from the cops . . . and . . . and he didn't."

"You sound sorry," Kurt accused. "You *wanted* him to get away, didn't you?"

They had finished eating, and Mr. Haley rose. He was watching the two boys uncertainly.

"We've all got a lot to think about. And a lot to be thankful for. We should remember these things in our prayers tonight."

"Anyway, Kurt sure has a lot of material for some new stories," Pat said, getting up and stretching her arms. "Except, I don't think we'll want to play them."

Kurt jumped up, his face flushed and angry. "I'll never write *anything* anymore." He stalked from the room.

"What on earth made him so angry?" Mrs. Haley asked, flinching when the upstairs bedroom door slammed. "He's so sensitive lately."

"It's all my fault," Pat said quickly. "I should never have mentioned anything about his stories because the convict made fun of them — he really did."

"Don't worry about it, Pat," said Mr. Haley. "Kurt's getting into the age where just about everything gets on his nerves. Now, everyone's had a long day, so let's go to bed and finish our stories of the big day some other time."

Jeff said nothing to Kurt when he got to the room they shared, but one look at his brother's face and he knew trouble was going to pop.

Kurt was sitting on his bed taking off his tennis shoes. "Well, Dad did it again."

"Dad? What are you talking about?"

"Whenever Dad doesn't know what to say, for or against, he gets out of it by saying we should remember these things in our prayers. Why can't he just come out and say something like, 'Hey, this is confusing. I kind of wanted the guy to get away too!' Or whatever he really feels."

"I don't think Dad had any doubts as to what to pray." Jeff slowly pulled off his own socks and shoes. He had that queer prickling feeling in his scalp that he got every time Kurt started talking about his "doubts" or anyone else's. Kurt was having more and bigger doubts all the time, and Jeff didn't like it. He had a few small doubts of his own, and he didn't think he was smart enough to tackle any big ones from a guy who was smarter and older than he was. Most of the time he just let Kurt do all the talking until he had talked himself dry, but when he said anything bad about Mother or Dad . . . well, that was too much for Jeff.

"Dad figured we each had our own things to pray and be thankful for," he began timidly.

"Oh, cut it! Dad didn't know whether to pray for the convict or not. If he did pray for him, what would he pray for — that the bum would suddenly get a big vision like — who was it, St. Paul — and get converted? Or should he have prayed that the convict got six more years in prison for making everyone chase around all night looking for him? He didn't know what to pray for, so he passed it off on us. How wishy-washy can you get?" He paused. "Tell me, what would you pray for, Jeff?"

But before Jeff could answer, Kurt went

on. "Dad could have just thanked God that we were all safe and sound inside our house, with our stomachs full of the quilters' goodies and that we were all such nice, honest kids and would never, *never* have to go to—"

"Oh, shut up!"

Kurt turned in utter surprise to look at his younger brother. He waited but Jeff said nothing more, climbed in his bed, and turned out his lamp.

Some time later Kurt said, "I'm sorry, Jeff, I get these doubts and they play over and over in my mind like a tape recorder. And I turn up the volume, and then you have to listen. You ever get doubts, Jeff?"

"Yeah, but not about Dad." Suddenly he sat up in bed and looked at his brother. "It's easy to sit there and let somebody else think up your prayers. Thataway you don't have to work at it at all. I guess Dad thought this was one time we'd better work at it."

"I guess you're right. I know Dad's great."

"You better believe it."

Long after Kurt was sound asleep, Jeff thought about the convict. It also bothered him that his brothers and sister seemed to take that long miserable day in the cave as though it had been just another cop and robber game that had turned out like always, with the good guys getting the bad guy. But to Jeff the day had been horribly real. The bad guy was not just playing a part, he was running from real cops with real guns. Right now he was in a hospital bed, and maybe there were guards at the door, bars at the window. Maybe the reason Jeff was the only one of them who realized what an awful day it had been was because he had seen the desperate fear in the boy's eyes before he started down that dark hole. A boy who was scared and *alone.*

"Jeff?"

"I thought you were asleep."

"I guess I was for a while, but I think I woke up especially to tell you that I was proud of you today."

"Thanks, Kurt."

CHAPTER 6

The next night Mr. Haley called a family court session in the living room.

"Your mother and I were talking about a new project. The back pasture is a fine level lot that isn't being used for anything. It would be large enough for a baseball diamond or a small football field—or even a place to work with my golf clubs—provided you took good care of them."

Pat went over to Mr. Haley's chair. "You don't have to worry about us playing cops and robbers again, Daddy."

"Never!" Jeff said with a shudder.

"Which of those cops was the deputy, Dad?" Donnie wanted to know. "So many of them stood around and watched, I didn't know."

Mr. Haley patted his head and went on with his own subject. "That land is covered with buckbrush, and I certainly can't afford to have some big machinery down here to dig it up, so you'll have to do it by hand. But I promise you this: if you boys pull out that brush, I'll get some men to help roll out the field, and we'll put up some good backstops."

"You could organize teams and have

friends out every Saturday, even when school starts." Mrs. Haley's eyes were sparkling. "I'll even furnish cookies."

"It would be great, but gosh, Dad, it'll take us weeks to pull that stuff up," Kurt grumbled.

"You start marking off a certain amount to be cleared each day, and you'll be surprised how soon it can be done. Pat and Donnie can help Mother with the indoor work while you two work outside."

Early the next morning Jeff and Kurt were standing exactly in the center of the area they had decided they would need to play baseball. They had stepped it off carefully so that each of them would have an equal amount of buckbrush to clear.

The pasture seemed to have enlarged overnight — it looked bigger than the airport in St. Louis and every inch of the ground was covered with buckbrush. Pat had once said she thought the weed was pretty with its shiny berries, but Pat hadn't known then that the weeds had roots clear down to China. The boys had tried to figure out how to get rid of the brush without wrestling those wiry roots by hand, but with no success.

"When do you think we'll get this place cleared?" Jeff sat back on his heels and yanked as hard as he could at a huge bush.

"When we get to be eighty." Kurt pulled up a small bush that surprised him by coming out so quickly that he staggered and fell back.

"Too bad that Sam won't be home until next week. We could have divided this into three sections and it wouldn't have been quite so awful."

Pat came out on the back porch drying a cup. "My, my, come look at the speed hounds, Mom. Look, they each have pulled up *one* bush."

"Want to trade jobs?" Kurt yelled.

"Oh, dear, no. I just joined the Inside Union, and I wouldn't dare work outside. But I don't think you divided the field the way you should."

"We measured off every step."

"I know that, but you should have gone by weight. Jeff doesn't weigh nearly as much as you do, Kurt, so he should have a much smaller piece of ground and . . ."

"Pat, please come in and finish the breakfast dishes," Mrs. Haley called. "Boys, you'd better get started. The sun is getting hotter by the minute."

"Let's try looking at the bright side," Jeff suggested. "Think of all the muscles we'll get yanking this stuff from mother earth."

"Right." Kurt tore furiously at a bush. "Come, come, dear mother earth, do let me have this bush. You have so many more growing other places."

"What an appetite we'll get! Think how good Mom's fried chicken will taste this noon."

They began to yank and pull and pile the brush on one side of the field.

"You talk about muscles—these plants have muscles of their own," Kurt grumbled.

"And they fight back too. Oh, well, you can't blame them. It's sort of a sad story. Buckbrush owned this land for years and years, and all the little animals and insects roamed and lived here, and everything was lovely. Now comes PROGRESS—that's us—and soon this lovely buckbrush forest will be beaten hard earth. And why? So that we can have a baseball diamond." Jeff finished breathlessly, a little proud of himself.

Kurt was surprised too. "It's poetry, kid, 'The Last Buckbrush.' It's enough to make you cry—or stop pulling the stuff." He yanked off his shirt and wiped his flushed face.

"Say, look, here's a big fine fat worm. Let's save him, and when we get our work done we can go fishing."

"That's a fine big juicy one. Why don't you go to the shed and bring back a can—also bring the thermos of water. I'm slowly drying up."

When Jeff came back with the water and an empty can, Kurt had found a place to rest under the shade of a tree near the fence.

"We need a break," he said. "Industry has discovered that people can put out more work if they have frequent rest periods."

"And who are we to argue against industry?" Jeff put the worm gently into the can and covered it with loose dirt.

"I'll bet the fish are biting in that place under the willows. We might catch enough to have a mess for supper." Kurt lay back and gazed at the misty white clouds that floated lazily across the sky.

Jeff watched the changing pattern of the clouds too, and his eyes were sad. "Suppose you had done something that was bad enough so that you had to be locked up."

Kurt got up. "You're worrying about that guy again. I think about him too — lots — but we don't really know the whole story, Jeff, do we? So turn down the tape recorder, we've got work to do." He began tugging at a huge weed.

Just then Jeff saw something move at the lower end of the pasture. It looked like some kind of animal, and it moved slowly in the higher brush. Jeff nudged Kurt. "Hey, do you see something moving down there? No, further over."

Kurt stared. "Yeah, I see it. What is it, a wild animal?"

The thing did not move very fast, but it was coming closer. Then they both saw its head, and they could hardly believe their eyes. It was a big black goat, and as he moved he was *eating buckbrush!* His little beard was moving up and down like mad, and he looked at the boys without any fear at all.

"He's eating it. He really is *eating* it down to the ground." Jeff wanted to run and hug the animal.

"Don't move," Kurt whispered. "He might stop and go away."

Slowly the boys sat down. They watched the goat eat the tough buckbrush just like a person eats celery, only much faster. The goat seemed to be enjoying it, but the boys hardly breathed for fear he would lose his appetite.

"If he doesn't fill up too soon, he'll have enough cleared for first and second base," Jeff said happily.

The goat was going through that patch as if he planned to down it all.

"Where do you suppose he came from? I've never seen a goat around here before." Jeff watched the black head, beard, and eyes and was reminded of a picture of a devil he'd once seen. "He looks like he stepped right up from hell."

"He's helping us out like an angel." Kurt snuggled down in the shade and watched his work disappear down the goat's throat.

"Hope he moves over to my side of the field pretty soon," Jeff worried.

Pat came out on the porch and the boys tried to signal her to be quiet, but as soon as she saw the goat she yelled out. "Mom, come here! There's a wolf with a beard in our back yard!"

Her yelling was loud enough to stampede a herd of buffalo, but the goat just looked up for a minute, then went right back to eating his buckbrush salad.

"I *do* love that goat," Jeff said as it moved over to his part of the pasture.

Mrs. Haley came out on the porch. "Well, did you ever?" she exclaimed. "A black goat! Look, he's eating buckbrush."

"Look at those lazy boys!" Pat said angrily. "They aren't doing a thing—just lying out there in the shade and letting that poor goat eat himself sick doing their work."

Mrs. Haley burst out laughing. "My goodness, look at that creature eat. Wonder where he came from?"

Pat didn't laugh. "I made lunch and I want you boys to come in and eat it so I can do the dishes and go to town with Mother to shop."

By this time the goat was just standing there chewing without eating, so the boys went inside. Pat's idea of making lunch was a couple of bologna sandwiches on a napkin and a glass of milk with two cookies.

"You said fried chicken," Kurt said reproachfully to Jeff.

"I didn't know Pat was going to do the cooking. *Cooking* — that's a laugh!"

"Maybe we should all drink out of the milk carton so poor overworked Pat wouldn't have all those nasty glasses to wash," Kurt said.

"Well, I don't happen to have a goat to eat my work," Pat blazed.

"Please, please!" Mrs. Haley begged. "Now, the agreement was to finish our work, then we all could do what we wanted for the rest of the afternoon. Donnie is helping Granny. Pat will be finished as soon as she cleans the kitchen. You boys get one-third of the buckbrush cleared and you're free."

"But the goat's doing it!" Pat protested.

"If they can get the goat to do it, it's all right with me."

Pat snatched at the glasses before the boys had finished their milk, and began slamming things in the sink with a lot of splashing.

When the boys went out to the pasture, the goat had wandered down to the wood patch and was eating there.

"This won't do," Kurt said. "We're going to have to get a long rope and tie him up here in the pasture so he eats where he's supposed to eat. Say!" He slapped his brother's shoulder in delight. "Then we can go down to the river and fish while he's eating up here!"

Jeff ran for a length of rope and they tried to stalk the goat. But the goat had other plans. He'd wait until they got almost up to him, then off he'd go. This went on and on and the boys got angrier and hotter by the minute. One time they had him cornered against the chicken house wall.

"We've got him!" yelled Jeff.

But that goat climbed right up the wall to the roof. They would never have believed it had anyone told them that goats could do that, but they *saw* it. There he stood on the roof above them, chewing.

"I'll try and lasso him — I'm getting pretty good. Sam and I work at it a lot," Kurt said.

"Go ahead," Jeff replied. "But watch so you don't get it too tight around his neck. We don't want anything to happen to his swallowing works."

However, Kurt's lassoing was so poor he couldn't even rope a bell-post by the barn. Even the goat must have gotten disgusted, because he came down off the roof and near enough for Kurt to grab him.

"This is no normal goat," Kurt said solemnly. "He's something from outer space. Imagine just coming up to be tied."

The boys tied the goat to a fence post in the shade with plenty of buckbrush all around him. They also put a big bucket of water nearby so he would not get thirsty. Then they got their fishing gear and worms and walked down to the river.

The fish weren't biting that day, but it was cool down by the river, and they spent the entire afternoon planning their baseball teams. It was late in the afternoon when they started back.

"Maybe we could lay out the bases tonight and call some of the guys for a game tomorrow," Kurt suggested.

They could hear some excited voices when they took the path to the back yard and saw the whole family outside. Granny had untied the goat, and it was standing beside her like they were the best of friends. Donnie and Pat were screaming so loud and fast no one could understand a word they said.

Kurt's and Jeff's hearts sank. There was just as much buckbrush in the pasture as when they had left for the river.

Then Pat's voice came through. "Our tennis shoes were standing out to dry, and that mean old goat *ate* them!"

"Just ate them all up—even the strings," Donnie added breathlessly.

Mrs. Haley looked stern. "Boys, do you know this goat ate most of the clothes on my line? You had no business leaving him here. He ate your father's new pajamas . . ."

"He ate the seat out of my new bathing suit!" Pat screamed, holding it up. "Look, *look!* He ate the whole seat out of it!" She burst into tears.

"This goat belongs to Mrs. Simmons," said Granny matter-of-factly. "He's a pet of hers and she usually keeps him tied up. She lives five miles up the road and I don't know how he got here, but she'll feel awfully bad about this, I know."

"We won't tell her," Mrs. Haley said. "It's the boys' fault. They should never have left that goat here alone. Now, boys, your father is going to expect a third of this yard to be done when he gets home, so you'd better get busy."

The buckbrush seemed to be growing in front of their eyes.

"Did you ever try digging around the roots of the big ones? They come up easier then," Granny suggested.

"Let's give up the baseball diamond. It's too hot, too hard, too much," Kurt said.

"We are not giving up the idea." Mrs. Haley's chin went up firmly, and that meant no

arguing. "To expect to get something worthwhile done without working is silly, and you might as well learn that now. Come on, Pat and Donnie, let's go inside and let the boys work. They have only a short time before their father comes home."

She took the few remaining things off the line, her face stern and angry.

"The whole seat's out," Pat wailed.

"I think I'll get new red tennis shoes." Donnie was the only cheerful one.

"I'll take the goat home," Granny said. Mrs. Simmons is coming down to pick up a quilt frame anyway."

"Don't tell her about the goat's meal," Mrs. Haley had to smile in spite of herself.

Just then Mr. Haley drove in the driveway. He waved a small package. "Look what I've got, Kurt."

Kurt opened the small box. "My watch," he exclaimed. "How did you get it, Dad?"

"I went to see the con—Ken Jarrit. He's doing fine. Had three broken ribs besides the fractured leg. He really seemed tickled to see me. He said to thank you for the use of the watch."

"But he didn't ask for it, he sto. . . ."

"Never mind, Donnie," Jeff broke in. "Why don't you think about those red tennis shoes."

Kurt slipped on the watch, a warm smile in his eyes. "I never thought I'd ever see this watch again."

Jeff smiled too. "I had my doubts."